T0365818

PAPA AND ME
WELCOME CHRISTOPHER TODD
AWAY WE GO! SPLISH! SPLASH!

Written by Grace

AuthorHouse™
1663 Liberty Drive
Bloomington, IN 47403
www.authorhouse.com
Phone: 1 (800) 839-8640

Published by AuthorHouse 02/16/2015

ISBN: 978-1-4969-6486-1 (sc)
ISBN: 978-1-4969-6487-8 (e)

Library of Congress Control Number: 2015900945

Scripture quotations marked KJV are from the Holy Bible, King James Version (Authorized Version). First published
in 1611. Quoted from the KJV Classic Reference Bible, Copyright © 1983 by The Zondervan Corporation.

Any people depicted in stock imagery provided by Thinkstock are models,
and such images are being used for illustrative purposes only.
Certain stock imagery © Thinkstock.

Print information available on the last page.

Because of the dynamic nature of the Internet, any web addresses or links contained in this book may have changed
since publication and may no longer be valid. The views expressed in this work are solely those of the author and do not
necessarily reflect the views of the publisher, and the publisher hereby disclaims any responsibility for them.

authorHOUSE®

Greetings Parents and Educators:

I decided to write the "Papa and Me" Series when I became a first time grandparent reflecting on my experiences and relationship with my grandson Cristen. It is a fictional reading book inspired by these experiences. This book is told from the eyes of a little boy shortly after his birth and later when he goes to live permanently with his grandparents. Your child will take the first exciting steps towards independent reading with the "Let's Read" books One, Two and Three. It includes the "Papa and Me" Series which offers the first three levels of reading: Beginning, Reading Together, and Independent Reading—each level contains fun stories reflecting Christian values with artistic drawings. Enjoy!

Let's Read, One, Two, Three!

Beginning Reading

1 Short sentences, easy words and word repetition, real-life illustrations.
Preschool-Kindergarten

Reading Together

2 Longer sentences, basic vocabulary, for children who recognize familiar words and sound out new words with help. Stories that engage for developing reading skills.
Preschool-Grade 1

Independent Reading

3 Attractive Topics, Stimulating Vocabulary, for children who are ready to read on their own.
Grades 1-3

I dedicate this book to
Alphonso Mosley, Jr.
who spoke to me about writing
a children's book, believing in me beyond
my own expectations. You've always
been a quiet friend to both Todd and I.

Philippians 2:3 Do nothing from selfishness or empty conceit, but with humility of mind regard one another as more important than yourselves.

WELCOME CHRISTOPHER TODD

WHAA! WHAA! WHAA!
Hey! What are you doing?

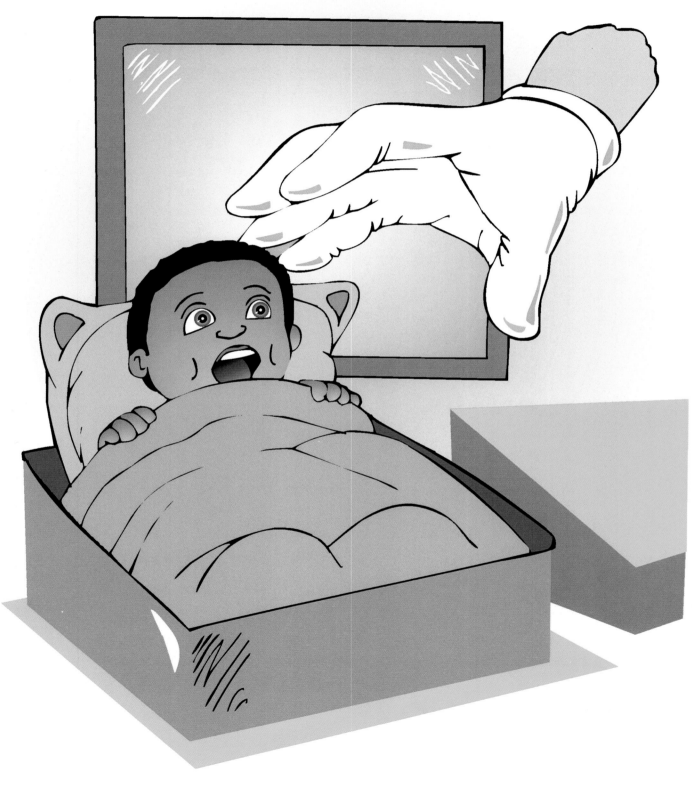

WHAA! WHAA! WHAA!
One finger, two fingers, three fingers four...
five, six, seven fingers and MORE...

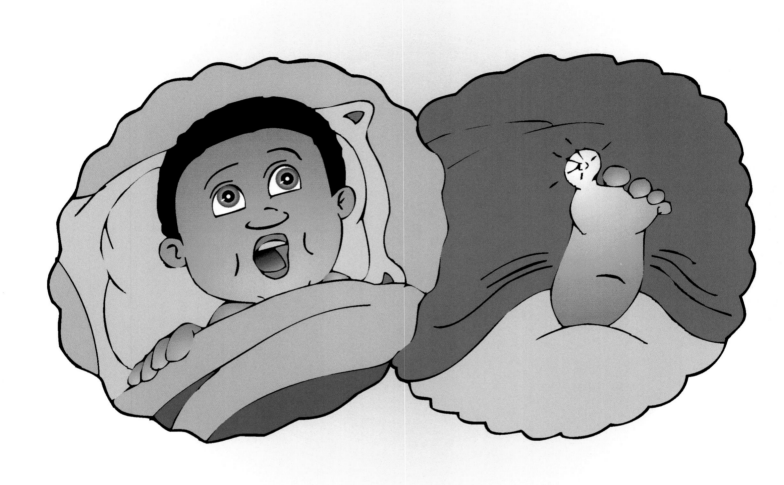

Eight, nine, ten!
Just a little prick…
WHAA! WHAA!

that's my Uncle Rick!

So many faces I see…
My Papa and Anaa all looking at me.

Everyone's looking; some just stare.
Who does he look like...
with his silky curly hair?

**Daddy's smiling and counting my toes.
Mommy looks like Papa
and I have Mommy's nose.**

Family! A circle of love,
like bright colored rainbows,
sweet as a white winged dove.

Smiles...

So much joy...
for the birth of a baby boy.

Here comes the lady in blue…
What will she do?
Will it be another prick?
I'll kick, kick, kick…

15

and cry, cry, cry.
WHAA! WHAA! WHAA!

There is Mommy and when she smiles...
she has holes in her cheeks
like me...
you see!

Balloons and bears all seem quite odd.
Just to show up with family to WELCOME
Me...
Christopher Todd.

Psalm 127:3-5 "*Behold, children are a heritage from the Lord, the fruit of the womb a reward. Like arrows in the hand of a warrior are the children of one's youth. Blessed is the man who fills his quiver with them! He shall not be put to shame when he speaks with his enemies in the gate.*"

AWAY WE GO!

Today I go to live with Papa and Anaa for awhile.

The family calls my grandmother Anaa.

AWAY WE GO!

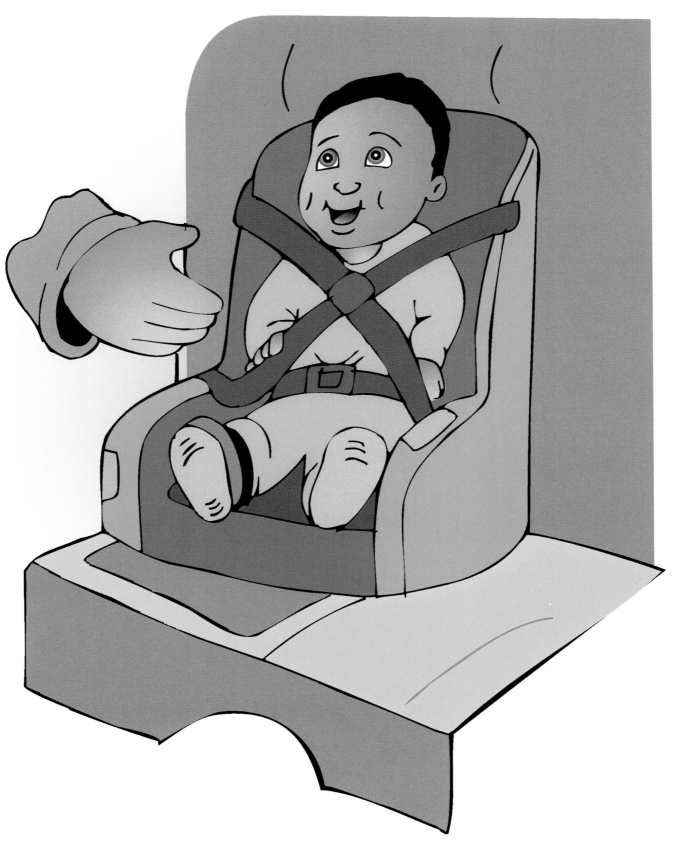

**Mommy
drives fast.**

**Mommy
drives slow.**

**Away to Papa and
Anaa's house we go!**

Clouds fly in the big blue sky.
Trees sway as mom drives far far away.

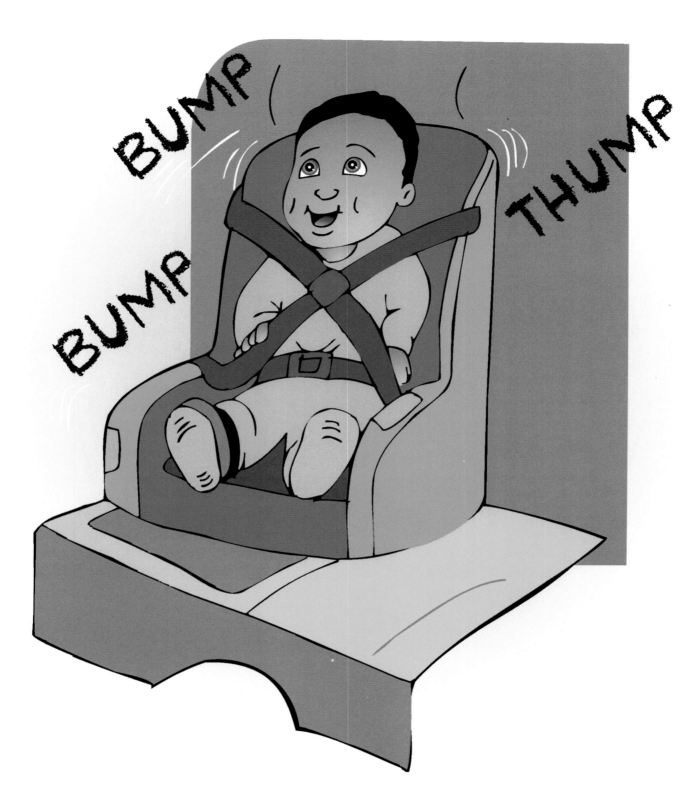

Bump! Bump! Thump! Thump!
The road thump and the car horn
Honk! Honk! Honk!

There's Papa and Anaa!

**I'm so special you see…
everyone does what's best for me.**

**Big tears, long hugs so
a little heart feels and knows…
why sometimes grandchildren
stay with grandparents …
and parents must come and go.**

Goodbye for now...
we won't be far away.
We will see you on weekends and make it a BIG day!

Psalm 103:17-18 *"But the lovingkindness of the LORD is from everlasting to everlasting on those who fear Him, And His righteousness to children's children, to those who keep his covenant and remember to do his commandments."*

Papa and I are in swim class.

**One, two peek a boo...
three, four
More! More!**

Here we go round the mulberry bush,
mulberry bush, mulberry bush
Here we go round the mulberry bush
all the way to town…

**Monday, Tuesday, Wednesday,
Thursday, Friday, Saturday,
Sunday...**

Splash!
Down, down in the water I go…
Wheee! Papa's hands are
what I know.

Splash! Splish!
and make a wish
one two
peek a boo

Learning to swim is fun to do.
I hold my breath...
no one tells me to.

Into the shower Papa washes my hair.
WHAA! WHAA! No fun in there.
There's no one two
or peek a boo.
No splash! Splish! or Splish! Splash!
No swish! Swish! or Swash! Swish!

**Dancing bears are in my head
as Papa put me down to bed.**

**Anaa comes in with teddy and a binky ring,
she smiled like mom and began to sing.**

Jesus loves me this I know.
For the Bible tells me so.
Little ones to him belong
They are weak but he is strong.

Yes, Jesus loves me.
Yes, Jesus loves me.
Yes Jesus loves me.
For the Bible tells me so.

Ephesians 6:1-4 *"Children, obey your parents in the Lord, for this is right. "Honor your father and mother" (this is the first commandment with a promise), "that it may go well with you and that you may live long in the land." Fathers, do not provoke your children to anger, but bring them up in the discipline and instruction of the Lord."*

PHONICS

see	kick	do	cry	thump
me	stick	to	why	bump
three		you	sky	honk
be		blue		
she				

slow	ring
know	sing
so	

Printed in the United States
By Bookmasters